Teaching Little Fingers to Play
Broadway Songs

Piano Solos with Optional Teacher Accompaniments arranged by
Carolyn Miller

Book

ISBN 978-1-4584-1765-7

Book/CD

ISBN 978-1-4584-1766-4

WILLIS MUSIC

EXCLUSIVELY DISTRIBUTED BY

HAL•LEONARD®
CORPORATION

7777 W. BLUEMOUND RD. P.O. BOX 13819 MILWAUKEE, WI 53213

Visit Hal Leonard Online at
www.halleonard.com

CONTENTS

Mini French lesson:

moi (mwa) – me
dites-moi (dit-a-mwa) – tell me
pourquoi (por-kwa) – why
piano – piano

Student Position

One octave higher when performing as a duet

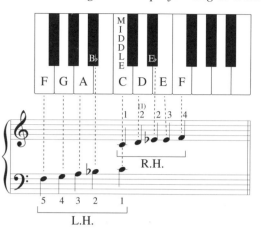

Dites-Moi

(Tell Me Why)

from SOUTH PACIFIC

Optional Teacher Accompaniment

Lyrics by Oscar Hammerstein II
Music by Richard Rodgers
Arranged by Carolyn Miller

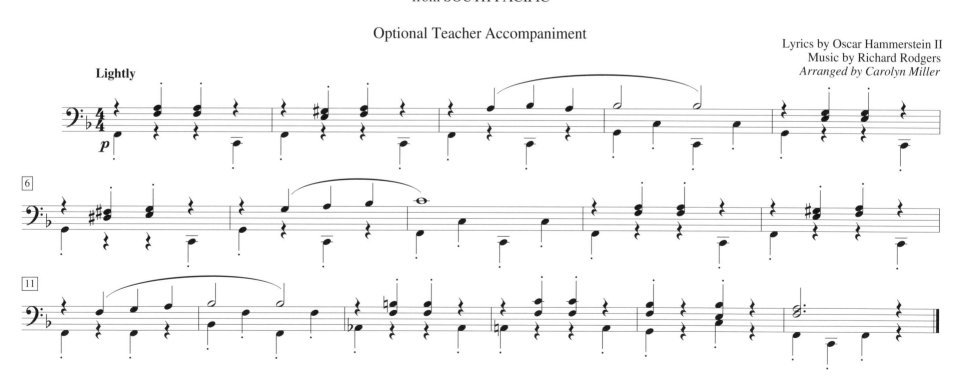

Dites-Moi
(Tell Me Why)
from SOUTH PACIFIC

Lyrics by Oscar Hammerstein II
Music by Richard Rodgers
Arranged by Carolyn Miller

TRACKS
1 – 2

Play both hands one octave higher when performing as a duet.

Lightly

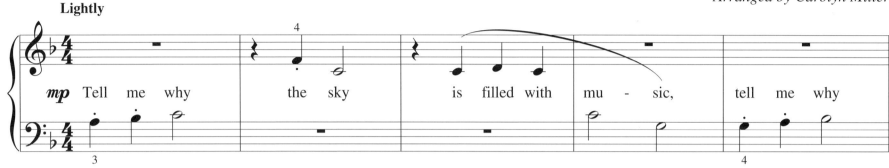

mp Tell me why the sky is filled with mu - sic, tell me why

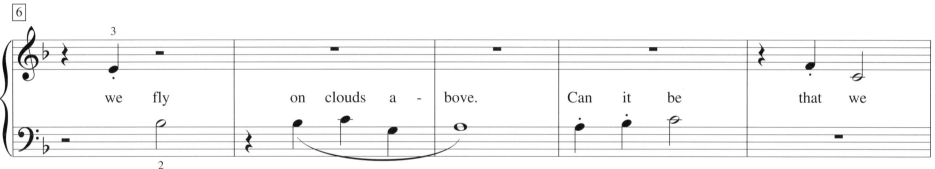

we fly on clouds a - bove. Can it be that we

can fly to mu - sic, just be - cause, just be - cause we're in love?

Did You Know?—
The popular musical *Annie* (and subsequent film) was based on a comic strip "Little Orphan Annie," created by Harold Gray, which began all the way back in 1924! (It recently ended in 2010.)

Student Position

One octave higher when performing as a duet

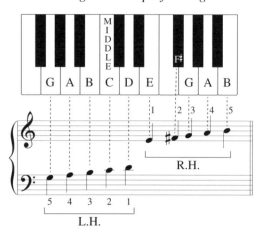

Maybe

from the Musical Production ANNIE

Optional Teacher Accompaniment

Lyric by Martin Charnin
Music by Charles Strouse
Arranged by Carolyn Miller

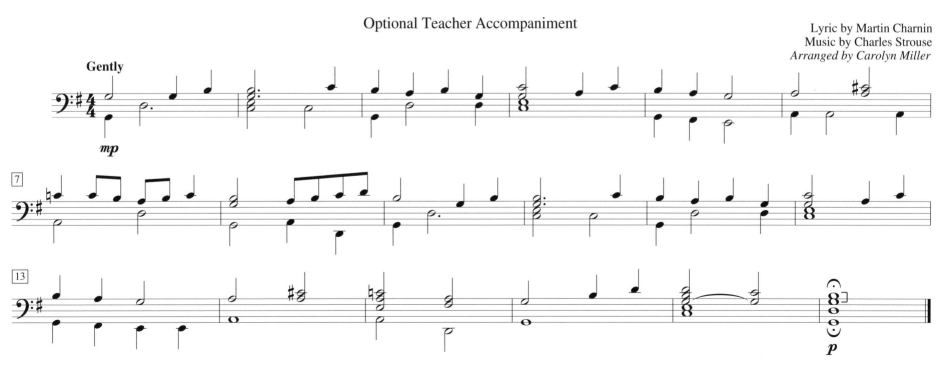

Maybe
from the Musical Production ANNIE

Lyric by Martin Charnin
Music by Charles Strouse
Arranged by Carolyn Miller

Play both hands one octave higher when performing as a duet.

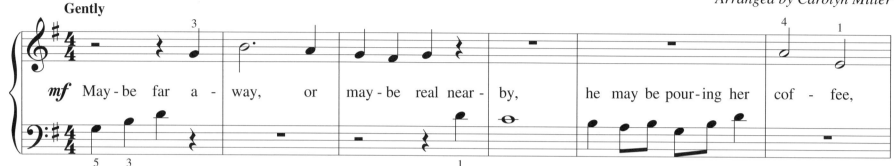

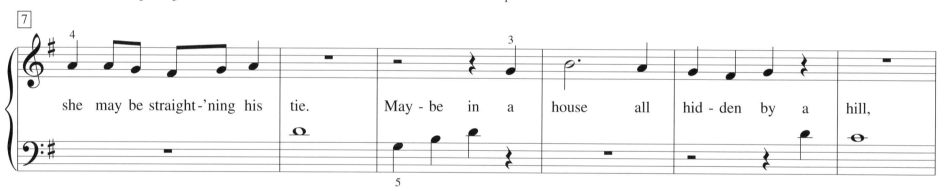

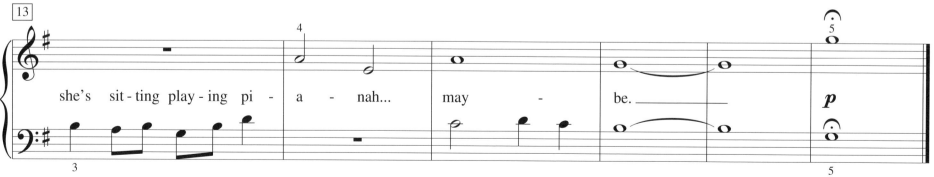

Did You Know?—

"Edelweiss" is one of the most beloved songs from *The Sound of Music*. It refers to a wooly white flower that grows high in the European Alps. According to German myth, young suitors would risk their lives and climb dangerous mountain cliffs to find the beautiful flower and bring it home to their sweethearts to prove the strength of their love.

Student Position

One octave higher when performing as a duet

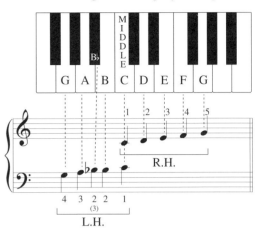

Edelweiss
from THE SOUND OF MUSIC

Optional Teacher Accompaniment

Lyrics by Oscar Hammerstein II
Music by Richard Rodgers
Arranged by Carolyn Miller

Edelweiss
from THE SOUND OF MUSIC

Lyrics by Oscar Hammerstein II
Music by Richard Rodgers
Arranged by Carolyn Miller

TRACKS 5 – 6

Play both hands one octave higher when performing as a duet.

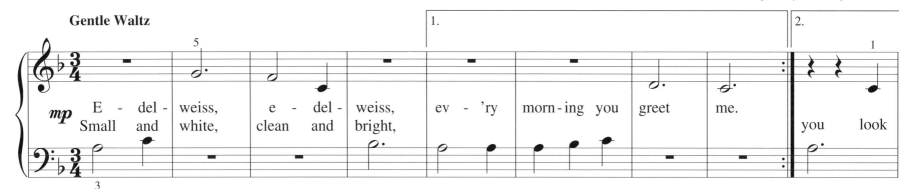

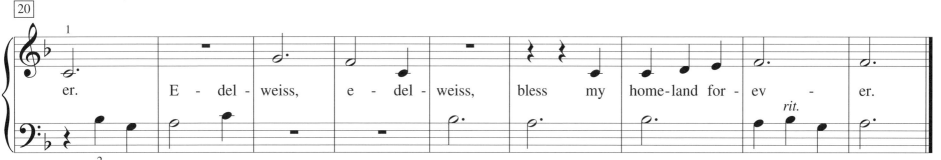

REVIEW—
A **half step** is the distance between any key and the next nearest key. A **whole step** is twice the distance of a half step: there is always one key – either black or white – lying in between. Circle all the half steps in this piece before starting to practice it.

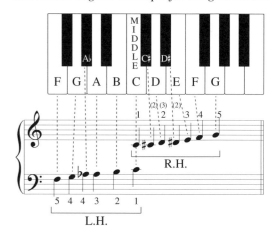

Student Position
One octave higher when performing as a duet

I Won't Grow Up
from PETER PAN

Optional Teacher Accompaniment

Lyric by Carolyn Leigh
Music by Mark Charlap
Arranged by Carolyn Miller

Happily, with a lilt

I Won't Grow Up

from PETER PAN

Lyric by Carolyn Leigh
Music by Mark Charlap
Arranged by Carolyn Miller

TRACKS
7 – 8

Play both hands one octave higher when performing as a duet.

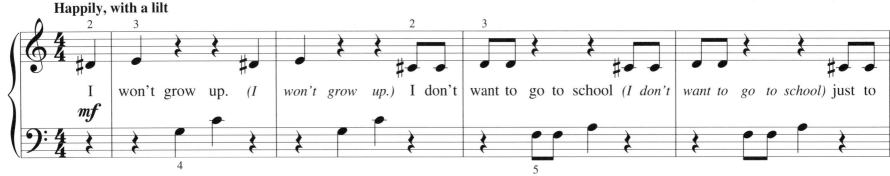

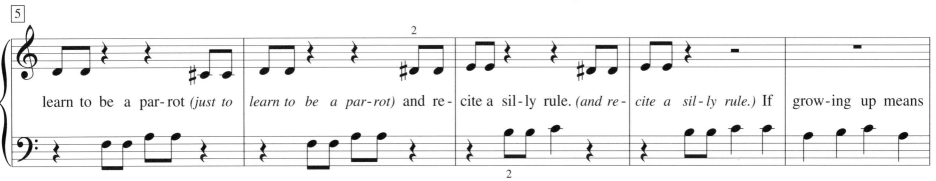

Did You Know?—

The Phantom of the Opera is the longest-running Broadway show of all time, opening in January 1988, and still going strong as of this writing a quarter of a century later.

Hint!—

Practice the last four measures of this piece carefully. Enjoy the unusual harmonies that lead up to the C Major triad.

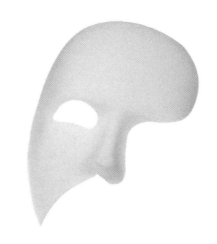

The Music of the Night
from THE PHANTOM OF THE OPERA

Optional Teacher Accompaniment

Music by Andrew Lloyd Webber
Lyrics by Charles Hart
Additional Lyrics by Richard Stilgoe
Arranged by Carolyn Miller

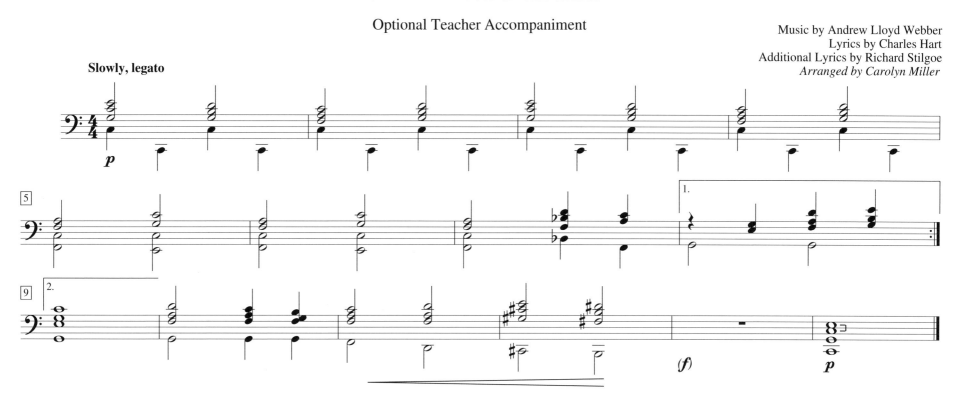

The Music of the Night
from THE PHANTOM OF THE OPERA

Music by Andrew Lloyd Webber
Lyrics by Charles Hart
Additional Lyrics by Richard Stilgoe
Arranged by Carolyn Miller

TRACKS
9 – 10

Play both hands one octave higher when performing as a duet.

Slowly, legato

Night-time sharp-ens, heighth-ens each sen-sa-tion; dark-ness stirs and wakes i-mag-i-na-tion.
Slow-ly, gen-tly, night un-furls its splen-dour; grasp it, sense it, trem-u-lous and ten-der.

Si - lent-ly the sens-es a-ban-don their de-fenc-es.
Turn your face a - way from the gar-ish light of day, turn your thoughts a - way from cold, un-feel-ing

light and lis-ten to the mu-sic of the night.

14

Did You Know?—
The composer of *The Music Man*, Meredith Willson (1902–1984), also played the flute and piccolo. He played in the New York Philharmonic Orchestra under Arturo Toscanini, and was also in John Philip Sousa's world-famous band.

Goodnight, My Someone
from Meredith Willson's THE MUSIC MAN

Optional Teacher Accompaniment

By Meredith Willson
Arranged by Carolyn Miller

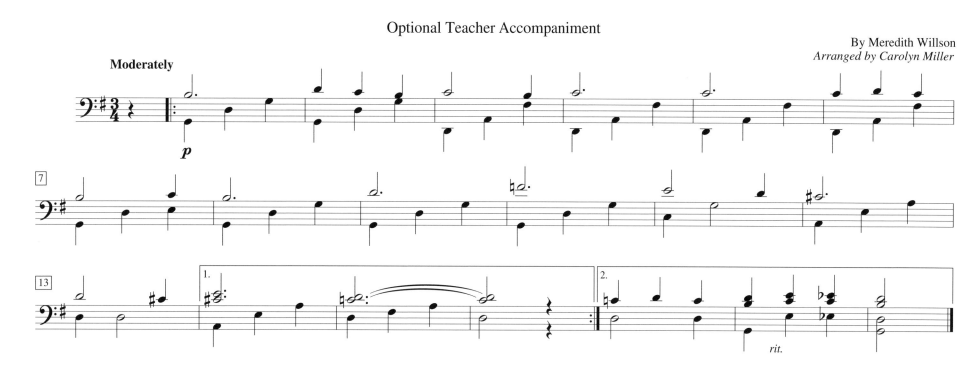

Goodnight, My Someone

from Meredith Willson's THE MUSIC MAN

TRACKS
11 – 12

By Meredith Willson
Arranged by Carolyn Miller

Play both hands one octave higher when performing as a duet.

Moderately

Did You Know?—
The musical *The King and I* is set in the Kingdom of Thailand (former name Siam) and is loosely based on the true story of British teacher Anna Leonowens, who was governess to the children of the legendary Thai King Mongkut (Rama IV) from 1862–1868.

I Whistle a Happy Tune
from THE KING AND I

Optional Teacher Accompaniment

Lyrics by Oscar Hammerstein II
Music by Richard Rodgers
Arranged by Carolyn Miller

I Whistle a Happy Tune

from THE KING AND I

Lyrics by Oscar Hammerstein II
Music by Richard Rodgers
Arranged by Carolyn Miller

TRACKS 13 – 14

Play both hands one octave higher when performing as a duet.

Optional Teacher Accompaniment

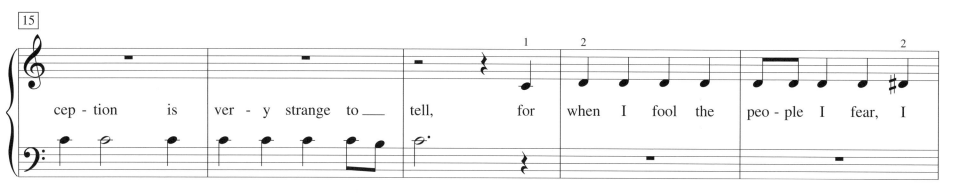

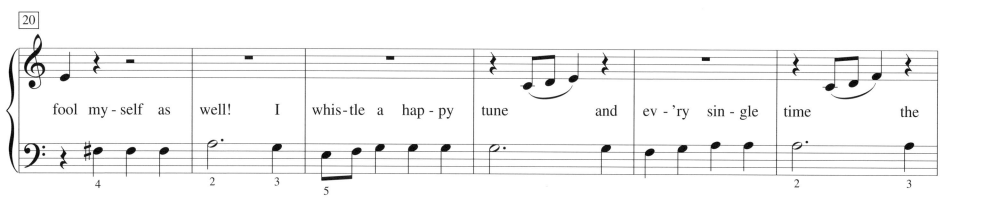

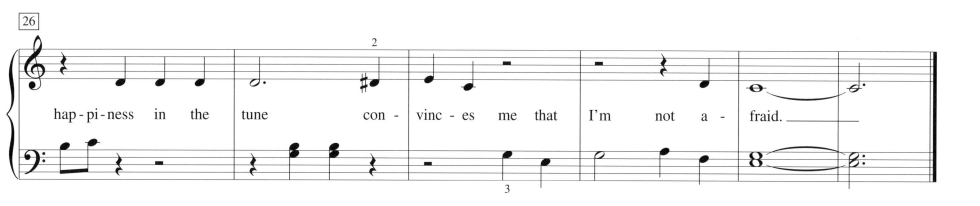

Did You Know?—
The Broadway production of *Oklahoma!* opened in 1943. Although it was a huge success, it did not win any Tony® Awards— the Tonys® were not yet in existence! The cheerful musical was Richard Rodgers and Oscar Hammerstein's first major success together.

Hint!—
There are several accidentals (sharp, flat, natural) in this piece. Find and circle them as you practice.

Out of My Dreams
from OKLAHOMA!

Optional Teacher Accompaniment

Lyrics by Oscar Hammerstein II
Music by Richard Rodgers
Arranged by Carolyn Miller

Out of My Dreams
from OKLAHOMA!

TRACKS 15 – 16

Lyrics by Oscar Hammerstein II
Music by Richard Rodgers
Arranged by Carolyn Miller

Play both hands one octave higher when performing as a duet.

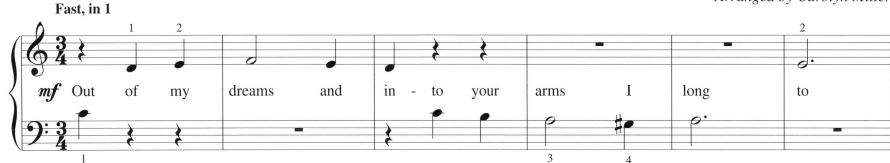

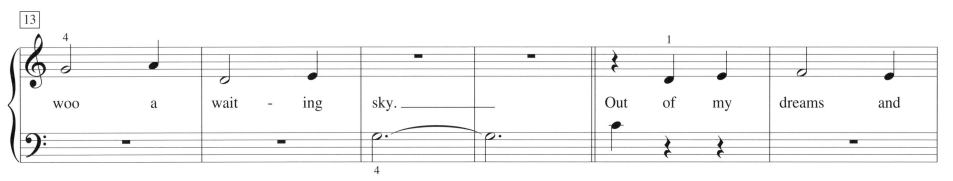

Optional Teacher Accompaniment

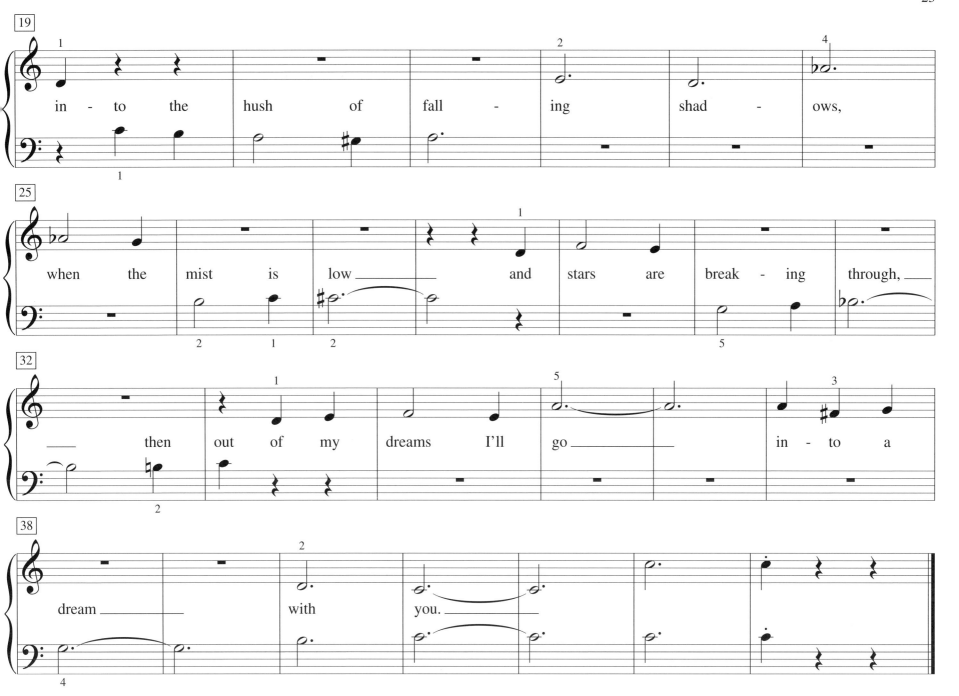

Did You Know?—
Big River is based on Mark Twain's classic *The Adventures of Huckleberry Finn*. The composer, Roger Miller, is still the only country artist to win a Tony® Award. (The musical won seven.) Another notable fact of the first Broadway production is that half of the performers (including the lead, Huck Finn) were portrayed by deaf or hard-of-hearing actors. Amazing!

Waitin' for the Light to Shine
from BIG RIVER

Optional Teacher Accompaniment

Words and Music by Roger Miller
Arranged by Carolyn Miller

Waitin' for the Light to Shine

from BIG RIVER

Words and Music by Roger Miller
Arranged by Carolyn Miller

TRACKS
17 – 18

Play both hands one octave higher when performing as a duet.

Slowly (in a folk-song style)

I have lived in the dark-ness for so long, I'm wait-in' for the light to shine.

Far be-yond ho-ri-zons I have seen, be-yond the things I've been, be-yond the

dreams I've dreamed are the things I've done. In fact, each and ev-'ry one are the

Optional Teacher Accompaniment

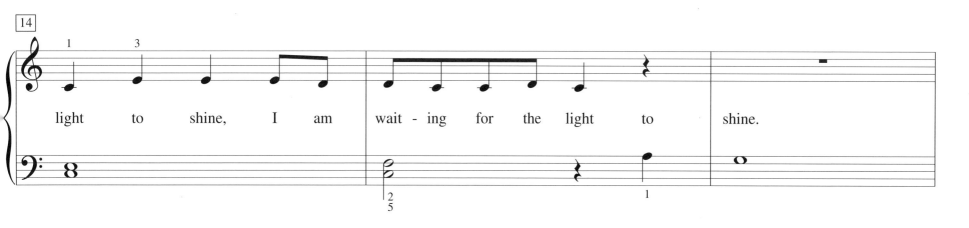

Did You Know?—
Based on the Charles Dickens classic, the musical *Oliver!* premiered on London's West End in 1960. Composer Lionel Bart was a prodigious talent, but could not read or notate music. In fact, the musical score was transcribed by Eric Rogers, who notated as Mr. Bart hummed the melodies to the songs!

Who Will Buy?
from the Broadway Musical OLIVER!

Optional Teacher Accompaniment

Words and Music by Lionel Bart
Arranged by Carolyn Miller

Who Will Buy?

from the Broadway Musical OLIVER!

TRACKS
19 – 20

Play both hands one octave higher when performing as a duet.

Words and Music by Lionel Bart
Arranged by Carolyn Miller

Quickly, with energy

Who will buy this won-der-ful morn - ing? Such a
Who will buy this won-der-ful feel - ing? I'm so

sky you nev - er did see. _____ Who will tie it
high, I swear I could fly. _____ Me, oh my, I

up with a rib - bon, and put it in a box for me?
don't want to lose it, and so what am I to

To Coda

Optional Teacher Accompaniment

TEACHING LITTLE FINGERS TO PLAY

JOHN THOMPSON'S MODERN COURSE
FOR THE PIANO

**TEACHING LITTLE FINGERS
TO PLAY**

A BOOK FOR THE EARLIEST
BEGINNER
COMBINING ROTE & NOTE APPROACH
"SOMETHING NEW IN EVERY LESSON"

W.M. Co. 5639

THE WILLIS MUSIC COMPANY
FLORENCE, KENTUCKY 41042

TEACHING LITTLE FINGERS TO PLAY
SONGS FROM MANY LANDS
International Songs for
the Earliest Beginner
Arranged by
Carolyn C. Setliff

THE WILLIS MUSIC COMPANY

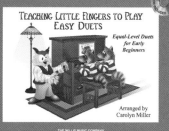

TEACHING LITTLE FINGERS TO PLAY
EASY DUETS
Equal-Level Duets
for Early
Beginners
Arranged by
Carolyn Miller

THE WILLIS MUSIC COMPANY

TEACHING LITTLE FINGERS TO PLAY
Disney TUNES
Delightful Disney Songs for the Earliest Beginner
Arranged by Glenda Austin
THE WILLIS MUSIC COMPANY

Disney characters and artwork are © Disney Enterprises, Inc.

TEACHING LITTLE FINGERS TO PLAY

A method for the early beginner combining rote and note approach. The melodies are written with careful thought and are kept as simple as possible, yet they are refreshingly delightful. All the music lies within the grasp of a child's small hands.

00412076 Book only	$4.99
00406523 Book/CD	$9.99

Foreign Language Editions

00414478 Book only (Spanish)	$4.99
00414498 Book only (French)	$4.95
00416444 Book only (Chinese)	$5.95

SUPPLEMENTARY SERIES

*All books are at the early elementary level and
include optional teacher accompaniments.*

CHILDREN'S SONGS
arr. Carolyn Miller

10 familiar melodies: "C" is for Cookie • Elmo's Song • The Hokey Pokey • How Much is that Doggie in the Window • On Top of Spaghetti • Puff the Magic Dragon • and more.

00416808 Book only	$6.99
00416809 Book/CD	$12.99

CHRISTMAS FAVORITES
arr. Eric Baumgartner

9 songs celebrating the season: Blue Christmas • The Chipmunk Song • Do You Hear What I Hear • I'll Be Home for Christmas • Rockin' Around the Christmas Tree • Silver Bells • and more.

00416721 Book only	$6.99
00416722 Book/CD	$12.99

CLASSICS
arr. Randall Hartsell

11 solos: Bridal Chorus (Wagner) • Can-Can (Offenbach) • A Little Night Music (Mozart) • Lullaby (Brahms) • Ode to Joy (Beethoven) • Swan Lake (Tchaikovsky) • and more.

00406550 Book only	$5.99
00406736 Book/CD	$10.99

DISNEY TUNES
arr. Glenda Austin

10 delightful Disney songs: The Bare Necessities • Candle on the Water • Kiss the Girl • Mickey Mouse March • Winnie the Pooh • Zip-A-Dee-Doo-Dah • and more.

00416748 Book only	$6.99
00416749 Book/CD	$12.99

FAMILIAR TUNES
arr. Glenda Austin

17 solos, including: Bingo • Buffalo Gals • If You're Happy and You Know It • I'm a Little Teapot • Lightly Row • Polly Put the Kettle On • Take Me Out to the Ball Game • and more.

00406457 Book only	$5.99
00406740 Book/CD	$10.99

HYMNS
arr. Mary K. Sallee

11 hymns: Amazing Grace • Faith of Our Fathers • For the Beauty of the Earth • Holy, Holy, Holy • Jesus Loves Me • Jesus Loves the Little Children • What a Friend We Have in Jesus • and more.

00406413 Book only	$5.99
00406731 Book/CD	$10.99

SONGS FROM MANY LANDS
arr. Carolyn C. Setliff

10 piano solos: Beautiful Dreamer • The Blue Bells of Scotland • Cielito Lindo • Du, Du, Liegst Mir im Herzen • Jasmine Flower • Little White Dove • 'O Sole Mio • On the Shore Across the Lake • Song of the Seasons • Sur le Pont d'Avignon.

00416682 Book only	$5.99
00416683 Book/CD	$10.99

Also available:

AMERICAN TUNES
arr. Eric Baumgartner

00406753 Book only	$5.99
00406792 Book/CD	$10.99

BLUES AND BOOGIE
Carolyn Miller

00406539 Book only	$5.99
00406727 Book/CD	$10.99

BROADWAY SONGS
arr. Carolyn Miller

00416926 Book only	$6.99
00416927 Book/CD	$12.99

CHRISTMAS CAROLS
arr. Carolyn Miller

00406391 Book only	$5.99
00406722 Book/CD	$10.99

CHRISTMAS CLASSICS
arr. Eric Baumgartner

00416825 Book only	$6.99
00416824 Book/CD	$12.99

EASY DUETS
arr. Carolyn Miller

00416830 Book only	$5.99
00416831 Book/CD	$10.99

JAZZ AND ROCK
Eric Baumgartner

00406572 Book only	$5.99
00406718 Book/CD	$10.99

JEWISH FAVORITES
arr. Eric Baumgartner

00416532 Book only	$5.99
00416670 Book/CD	$10.99

RECITAL PIECES
Carolyn Miller

00416539 Book only	$5.99
00416672 Book/CD	$10.99

EXCLUSIVELY DISTRIBUTED BY

WILLIS MUSIC

HAL•LEONARD®
CORPORATION
7777 W. BLUEMOUND RD. P.O. BOX 13819
MILWAUKEE, WISCONSIN 53213

Complete song lists online at **www.halleonard.com**
Prices, contents, and availability subject to change without notice.